Shaasha Barta

Shaasha Barta

✦

The Book of the 41 Virtues

Tika

iUniverse, Inc.
New York Lincoln Shanghai

Shaasha Barta
The Book of the 41 Virtues

All Rights Reserved © 2004 by Tika ni Tua

iUniverse, Inc.

For information address:
iUniverse, Inc.
2021 Pine Lake Road, Suite 100
Lincoln, NE 68512
www.iuniverse.com

ISBN: 0-595-28975-4

Printed in the United States of America

This book is dedicated to my mother Louise Perez-Jones without whose wisdom, selfless support and encouragement, this work could not have been completed. Also to my father George Jones whose appreciation for African art and aesthetics ultimately became a part of me. And finally, to my maternal grandfather Tiburcio "Thomas" Perez, a great man of Garifuna heritage who deliberately and lovingly imbued me with an appreciation for and commitment to the values of a more elegant past.

Contents

Acknowledgements

I'd like to thank Larry Cross who first suggested that I write this book. I'd also like to thank Erriel Kofi Addae whose thoughtful suggestions made this a better work. This effort would have been considerably more difficult without the support and assistance of family members including my wife Karen, my brother Thomas Jones and most particularly my sister Jessica Colley whose assistance with the editing process was invaluable. There have also been many individuals too numerous to name who have provided encouragement throughout this process. And to them, my deepest thanks.

Introduction

During the colonial era in Kenya and Tanzania, British officials often arrested and jailed young Maasai warriors for traditional activities now deemed criminal. After reviewing the practice, they decided to discard it, selecting instead to charge fines for warriors' "transgressions". The reason for this decision was that they soon realized that by jailing these young warriors of the plains, they were in fact issuing death sentences.

Their sense of freedom was so strong that imprisoned Maasai warriors would refuse food and water and in their forlorn misery chose death rather than spend months unable to see the crimson sun rise over the grassy East African plains. Today, there are literally hundreds of thousands of Black males, related through African heritage to these Maasai warriors, who have come to see prison as their second home. Many prefer prison to the uncertainty and harshness of the outside world.

The reason many of our young people are conflicted about choosing between prison and the outside world is that they cannot discern a meaningful difference between the two. Freedom comes from a sense of purpose in life and a belief in your own ability to accomplish that purpose. True freedom for a warrior comes when he knows that he has done all within the awesome power of his being to serve his people while walking a righteous path through life.

As a people, we have taken a page from the book that says, "When in Rome, do as the Romans do", forgetting that the Romans perished under the weight of their own depravity and decadence. Western society attacks Black males for behaving in a manner out of step with ideals of morality. Sober minds realize, however, that this same society has created a mode of conduct that is far out of step with traditional African culture.

Sidney Hinde wrote, "The Maasai are quick at learning. As a race [sic] they are intelligent and truthful and a grown Maasai will never thieve or lie. He may refuse to answer a question but, once given, his word can be depended on." [1]

The African concept of warriorhood was a moral humanistic one. It guided young men toward a path of high levels of service to their community. While this values driven system sought to create security and order within each community, it also took pains to ensure a sense of humaneness toward other cultures, even during warfare. Warriorhood in Africa was not kill centered.

In European cultures, the idea of killing was the central theme around which everything else revolved. The Vikings, for example, had a concept called "berserksgangr" from which we get the word "berserk". This concept in essence, equated killing with sexual ecstasy. In other words, the taking of life was perceived as orgasmic in proportion. Such a concept is thoroughly anti-African in nature.

The first institution destroyed during the Maafa (Great Suffering) was the age-grade system, which passed along ideas of morality, decency, compassion and correct behavior. The problem that this created for the slavery system was that it also deliberately fostered a sense of responsibility for the safety and protection of one's people. This made it necessary for slave holding societies to destroy it and anything that could lead to its resurrection.

One charge leveled against Black males is that they are too concerned with their manhood. Criticism of Black manhood is based on a lack of understanding of the true concept of manhood. The late Dr. Amos Wilson, a psychologist who wrote numerous books on the crisis facing Black males pointed out that manhood in Africa is a nurturing concept. In traditional culture, in order to be a man, one had to be the ultimate nurturer.

This meant that a man was expected to give and never to take from society. The warriors had to make sure that there was enough food for everyone to eat. A warrior's major concern was to provide safety and security for each person in his society. In this way, everyone within society had a feeling of peace. Male elders were required to provide guidance, not only to their own children but to all of the young men in their society.

The "manhood" concepts presently practiced by Black males are taken from those who created our current condition. The result is a form of manhood that is predatory, dependent, exploitive and self-destructive and contributes nothing to the common good. Instead of setting up a safe environment for the people within their community, it destroys any chance of security. At the same time it provides safety for those who seek to exploit and control from without.

There was enormous power in the process of making a man in traditional culture. Travelers through the continent recognized this and were impressed enough to comment. One for example, referring to the Dinka wrote, "The Dinka...is a gentleman. He possesses a high sense of honor, rarely telling a lie...I must add a rare dignity of bearing and outlook." [2]

While there were times when atrocities did occur, such as during the reign of Shaka Zulu, they were rare. Even Shaka's contemporaries considered him to be insane although great and this perception ultimately led to his violent overthrow by his own family.

We see also, that in the great West African empires of the savannah where mighty battles were fought, there were humanistic rules in place. Harold Courlander writing about the Bambara kingdom of Segu informs us that, "The chivalric code was observed not only in individual combat, but also in wars between armies. An attacking army might make an 'appointment' with its adversary, announcing a 'visit' on a certain day. Arriving at the walls of the adversary's city, the attackers would extend courteous greetings and receive greetings in return...If the defending city was not ready to begin fighting, the attackers waited patiently in their camps. Battles usually began at daybreak and continued until nightfall. If an attacking army arrived at a city's walls in late afternoon, it was too late to begin and the fighting was deferred until the next morning. Meanwhile, the attackers were invited inside the city for an evening of feasting and drinking and before daybreak they would return to their camp, take up their weapons and prepare for battle." [3]

Among east African nomadic cultures where warfare took the form of cattle raids to increase their herds, again the taking of life was not a central aim.

"War was not a cause of social upset, or a crisis; it was a period of intensified living, a phenomenon which was institutionalized and integrated into the economic and political organization. Thus among the Maasai, who live in Kenya and Tanzania in the Kilimanjaro area, when the members of a band of warriors planned a raiding expedition, they asked the local chief to lay out a plan of attack and eventually to obtain the cooperation of other bands...When consent was given, the warriors prepared themselves by feasting on meat; scouts were sent out, and the expedition began. Expeditions were carried out against the neighboring tribes, and sometimes went as far as the coast, more than 250 miles away...These expeditions did not result in the loss of many human lives. The same was true when large Maasai armies fought among themselves." [4]

At the core of African warriorhood tradition is a high moral standard, which is inculcated into the education of the young initiate. This is expected to remain with a man throughout his lifetime. At a Maasai ceremony of graduation into elderhood filmed for PBS, several elders address the graduates, reminding them of their duties.

1ˢᵗ elder: "From now on, forget the rough ways of moranhood (warriorhood). Don't be rude to junior elders, or to any

woman. Take with you the good influences of this ceremony."

2nd elder: "Go home and respect your people. Respect is the most
important thing on earth."

3rd elder: "We are your moral guardians and we take our duties
very seriously." [5]

Francis Mading Deng writing about his people the Dinka, illuminates their tradition.

"Dinka concepts of unity and harmony are expressed in "cieng". As a noun it means morals, behavior, habit, conduct, nature of custom, rule, law, way of life or culture. Although some of these concepts may not show it clearly, cieng is a concept of human relations. It puts values like dignity and integrity, honor and respect, loyalty and piety, and the power of persuasiveness at its core." [6]

In looking again at the Bambara where the concept of chivalry had reached its zenith, we see a connection in the behavior of the knights.

"All nobles and heroes foremost, were governed by a code of chivalry probably unsurpassed in the traditions of other peoples. When heroes came together, a number of courtesies were observed…It was considered dishonorable for a noble to fight someone whom he knew to be afraid of him. If he discovered his opponents fear before challenging him, he would not make the challenge. If he made the discovery at the moment of combat he would turn and ride away…sometimes a young hero declined to fight an elder man who resembled his father." [7]

The idea of duty to one's people or society was the all-important context of the warriors' existence. There was, however, a great deal of room for individuality. Individual warriors and knights competed to distinguish themselves in boldness, courage, adherence to duty and honor. For those who achieved distinction, the rewards were numerous and varied. For the truly outstanding, a permanent place would be won in the legends and songs of the people.

An observer traveling through Maasai territory during the early part of the century witnessed a Maasai lion hunt pulled together after a lion had stolen some cattle.

"Suddenly the tip of the lion's tail began to twitch. One! Two! Three! Then he charged for the ring of spearsmen. At once half a dozen spears leaped through the air towards him…The lion never paused in his stride. In his path stood one of the moran, a youngster on his first hunt. The boy never flinched. He braced himself to meet the charge, holding his shield in front of him and swaying back slightly so as to put the whole weight of his body into his spear thrust. The lion sprang for the boy. With one

blow he knocked the young moran's (warrior's) shield out of his hand as though it were cardboard. Then he reared up trying to sweep the boy toward him with his out-stretched paws.

The boy drove his spear a good two feet into the lion's chest. The mortally wounded beast sprang on him, fixing his hind claws in the boy's belly to insure his grip while at the same time he seized the boy's shoulder in his jaws.

The young warrior went down under the weight of the great cat. Instantly all the other moran were around the dying lion. It was too close for spears. The men used their double-edged simis, heavy knives about two feet long...I examined the wounded boy. His wounds were truly frightful yet he seemed completely indifferent to them. I sewed him up with a needle and thread. He paid no more attention to the process than if I were patting him on the back."[8]

In addition, we're told, *"The Maasai believe that the bravest act a man can per-form is to grab a lion by the tail and hold the animal so the other warriors can close in with their spears and simis. Any man who can perform this feat four times is given the title of melombuki and ranks as a captain. It is also an unwritten law among them that any man who gains this title must be willing to fight anything living."*[9]

Another writer relates an incident where lions had been attacking the cattle of another people called the Lumbwa, neighbors of the Maasai and also known for the prowess of their warriors. A single warrior decided to search for the culprits alone.

"He stood up and stamped his foot and called 'Ha!' But the lion, who put first things first, went on eating. So the moran drew back his spear arm and shot the blade. It slashed the flank of the lion, which, still putting first things first, now went into a charge.

The Lumbwa took it on his hide shield, going back and over, with his sword stab-bing, and the lion's claws at his shoulders, until the lion was dead with the soft iron inside him, and the moran had done no more than his people would expect of a war-rior."[10]

This kind of selflessness could be seen throughout the continent in a large number of societies. Writing about the Zulus, E.A. Ritter demonstrates this fact.

"The spirit of joviality, comradeship and esprit de corps ever strong in the African nature, was here at its best. While ease and freedom were enjoyed, stern discipline con-tinuously reigned; but it was a wholly moral force, the young men being thrown entirely upon their honor, without standing regulations and without supervision; and they seldom dishonored that trust. They were there for the sole purpose of fulfilling the king's behests. They acted as the State army, the State police, and the State labor gang. They fought the clan's battles, made raids when the State funds were low...they slew

convicted, and even suspected malefactors and confiscated their property in the king's name; they built and repaired the king's kraals (cattle pens); cultivated his fields and manufactured his war shields; for all of which they received no rations, no wages, not one word of thanks. It was their duty to the State as men, and they did it without question or complaint." [11]

For the Hadendoa, the famous and fierce cloaked warriors of the battle for the Sudan, leaders were chosen based on whether they possessed a good reputation, wisdom, a sense of humor, hospitality and oratorical skill. Honor, face keeping and modesty were vital elements in their code of conduct. A real Hadendoa must be responsible and maintain his sense of honor by being self-controlled, brave and able to protect the women and children as well as guests from physical harm. Every man was also responsible for the maintenance of honor in his community. A man was expected to bend over backwards in providing for the comfort of a guest, continually checking to see that all of his or her needs were met.

Clearly, Africans throughout the world are at a crossroads. Misinformed, ashamed, confused and misguided, the sons of Africa must choose between what has been thrust upon them, the slow lingering death of collapsed values. Or, a chance at redemption through the retaking of ideals and ways of life which once gave strength.

The barta or covenant with the ancestors has been broken, producing a wasteland through which blow the winds of immorality, desolation and decay. Shaasha Barta is intended as an oracle, restating an ancient wisdom with the power to address problems facing Black men in the difficult world in which they live. It is offered as a key to confronting the confusion generated by the storm that swirls mercilessly across the land leaving ruin in its wake.

It is neither a religious doctrine nor a dogma, but a blueprint for a way of life with the spiritual force necessary to offer guidance through the stress and uncertainties of daily living. Thus established, it opens a path by which the greater good can be served.

A Word About the Text

The 41 principles of the Shaasha Barta are based on traditional African concepts of morality and behavior specifically as they pertain to the inculcation of warriorhood values in traditional societies. They are not intended as word-for-word renderings of a set of principles. They are instead designed to give Black males a set of principles completely based on a traditional foundation that speaks specifically to the unique environment and attendant conditions with which they grapple on a day-to-day basis.

Shaasha Barta translates to Respect Covenant in Kemetic (ancient Egyptian). The Kemetic language is related culturally and linguistically to an astonishingly large number of African societies. It seemed fitting to use such an ancient and important language that also prided itself on its values and morality to title the principles of the text.

Each principle is highlighted on the left by a corresponding legend, quote or set of proverbs that relate to the theme of the individual principles. Care was taken so that the highlighting legends and proverbs were either in their original forms or condensed from the form in which the Africans told them themselves. Pains were taken not to include highlights of the precepts as "interpreted" by non-Africans although this would have made the task infinitely easier. Literal translations were used as well as quotes.

The effect is of an ancestral oracle, offering light to those in need of guidance, encouraging them to face the challenge of life as the warriors of old times would have. It is to this purpose that the Shaasha Barta is meant to serve and to this end that the text dedicated.

Some Cultures Cited in the Text

<u>Maasai</u> A people inhabiting Kenya and Tanzania with a cattle based economy and culture. One of the better known African cultures, the Maasai were reknowned for their aggressiveness. It is said that their reputation was such, that Arab slaving caravans gave a wide berth to their territory to avoid encountering them.

<u>Yoruba</u> Based in modern Nigerian, the Yoruba founded several powerful city-states. The Yoruba had a vigorous culture, which gave birth to some of the finest art as well as a complex religion with adherents throughout the new world.

<u>Beja/Hadendoa</u> Known to the Romans as the Blemmeyes, the Beja are one of the most ancient cultures. The Hadendoa are the most numerous branch of the Beja. Known as powerful and fierce warriors who distinguished themselves in the battle with the British for control of the Sudan during the Mahdiya uprising. Easily recognized by their cloaks of cotton fabric and large Afro hairstyles, these camel riding and breeding nomads once controlled the northern trade routes.

<u>Bambara</u> Once ruling a large area of West Africa, the Bambara became powerful after the fall of the Songhay empire. Their first kingdom Segu was founded by hard riding bandit horsemen who eventually settled down and began the process of empire building with a strict set of laws and a refined system of law and order. They exist today primarily in the nations of Senegal and Mali.

<u>Abyssinia</u> Subsequently known as Ethiopia, an empire comprising many cultures was the last African empire to fall to Western imperialism (they were not defeated until World War II). Abyssinia has a long proud history. They have their own script called Ge'ez and their ruling families once traced their lineage to the Queen of Sheba and Solomon.

<u>Ganda</u> Sometimes known as the Baganda, they were a dominant force in the Great Lakes region now known as Uganda. Beginning in the mid 1600's under an energetic and determined warrior king, Katerega, the Ganda expanded their frontier incorporating many of their neighbor states into their empire. They possessed a well organized army unequaled in the region except by Nyoro.

<u>Dinka</u> The Dinka were and are a fiercely independent people. They are the most numerous ethnic group in Sudan. They call themselves Monyjang or Men

of Men. Throughout history they have proudly resisted outside invasion and interference with their culture.

Wodaabe The Wodaabe are a branch of the populous Fulani or Peul of West Africa. They are nomadic cattle herders who have maintained very ancient traditions of morality and behavior. The Fulani once controlled vast empires on horseback and at times allied themselves with other strong neighbors to secure their holdings.

Gikuyu An East African culture found in Kenya. They were chiefly responsible for and the main participants in the so-called Mau-Mau uprising which led to the overthrow of the British and the installation of Jomo Kenyatta, himself a Gikuyu. They were in earlier times part of the cattle complex of the region and held their own against strong cultures such as the Maasai in the carving out of grazing lands on the plains.

Nyoro The Nyoro kingdom, founded around 1500 in present day Uganda under the Bito ruling dynasty soon made its presence felt throughout the region. Their dominion spread even over the Ganda who did not become a major power in their own right until some 150 years later. They were wealthy in cattle, which, as with many African states were the center of the agricultural economy.

Benin The Bini or people of Benin were known for extraordinary skill in metalworking, particularly brass and bronze and beautiful sculpture. They once controlled a huge area from modern Lagos, Nigeria to the Niger delta.

Zulu One of the most famous and well known warrior cultures. Starting as a small and insignificant clan of the Nguni people it was transformed into a hardened martial empire by its king, Shaka. Under his aggressive expansionist policies, they extended Zulu rule over much of Southern Africa until he was deposed violently by his family. The Zulu later became a major threat to British interests in Southern Africa.

Dogon One of the most ancient cultures on the continent dating back to at least 500 B.C., the Dogon entered the Great Niger Bend after driving out the Tellem peoples in the fifth century B.C. For much of their history they've been threatened by powerful peoples—the Songhay in the north, the Hausa in the east and the Mandinka in the west. They are less known for militarism than for their highly structured philosophical and religious strength. Western astronomers have been baffled at how they discovered the existence and orbital paths of certain stars before they were known to Europeans.

Bushongo A people of central Africa most known for the legacy of the 17th century philosopher king Shamba. The Bushongo like other peoples of the region used a version of the heavy throwing knife shaped like a bird of prey. Shamba outlawed the use of these and other deadly weapons in the interest of furthering a more humane way of life.

Kanuri People of the Kanem-Bornu Empire. They were known for their restless campaigns of expansion on horseback, which ultimately gained a vast stretch of territory and subject nations in the west African savannah region. Their empire lasted even longer than those of Mali and Songhay.

"…And if even the heavens should hold over us a threat to fall and crush us, we shall take our spears and prop it up."

—Gikuyu

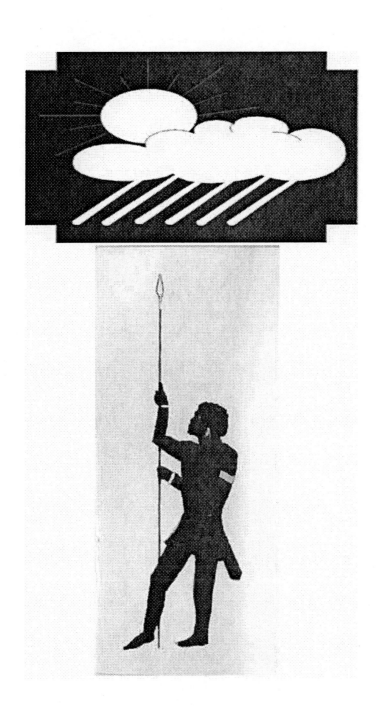

"Have courage. Timidity and cowardice are for men who can see safety at their backs or retreat without molestation and find refuge in the familiar fields of their native lands but they are not for you. You must be brave."

—*Hannibal Barca of Carthage, North Africa addressing his troops after his successful invasion of Rome.*

Courage

Selfless courage is the creed of the warrior. Courage will be the only true wall of defense between yourself and those who oppose you. Let not concern for personal enrichment be the sole governing force in your life. The strength and resolve of your spirit will drive your cause to victory.

Questioner: '"When will the warriors be allowed to marry?'

Shaka: 'Marriage for young warriors is folly. Their first and last duty is to protect the nation from its enemies. This they cannot do efficiently if they have family ties. When they reach a mature age, and have proved their worth, I am prepared to consider individual cases, and even whole regiments, if they have shown exceptional merit. But until the nation has been made secure against all external enemies, the marriage ban will be strictly enforced on all warriors…'"

—*From a Zulu "free speech" ceremony where the people were permitted to ask any question of King Shaka Zulu.*

Protect

Protect your people as you would yourself and, when necessary, go beyond what you would do for yourself. Create peace and harmony in your environment, and the blessings will be evident in your behavior and those whom you strive for. Maintain respect for the sanctity of life, and reverence for the great temple under the sky called earth.

While conquest lies in the realm of the marauder,

Victory dwells within the domain of the just.

Ye, to this truth we pledge our fealty,

And to this truth we rise as one.

Abyssinian military commander Dames Nasibu.

"King Esigie came to the throne a young and impetuous man. He had not as yet acquired the wisdom of maturity. The people had no respect for him due to his insensitivity and irresponsibility.

One high-ranking official who had suffered greatly from one of Esigie's practical jokes encouraged the king of Idah to attack hoping to end Esigie's reign. An old priest went through the streets of Benin telling the young warriors that an attack on the city did not affect the king alone, but would cause them and their loved ones to suffer as well. Finally they listened.

They set up camp that night to rest before the final assault. Just then, an ibis flew across the face of the full moon out that night—a very bad omen.

The next morning, the troops refused to go into battle, resolved that they would lose anyway. Esigie ordered his generals to saddle his horse. He mounted and said to the men, "If you will not give me your support, I will go on alone and face the Idah in battle."

For the first time they saw someone they could respect. A brave young man full of spirit. They saw a man in possession of dignity and honor. A hero. They marched forth, defeating the Idah decisively.

Esigie waited at his mother's birthplace for the people to forgive him. Out of respect for the courage he displayed on the battlefield, they forgave him and welcomed him back to Benin. He returned a much wiser and humbler man and his reign was long and prosperous."

—*From the Three Rivals, one of the legends of the Benin kings.*

Humility

May the people you serve speak confidently of your virtues, for this is the truest measure of your devotion to them and thus, the measure of your merit as a warrior. Each black woman is your mother, sister or daughter and each black man your father, brother, son. Callousness toward your people is at once unnecessary and immoral and has no place in the world of the true warrior.

"When you are a child you don't know much. But as a moran (warrior) you become more clever. You visit new places far away. You get to know how to defend yourself and you mature. Moranhood is very good. It's a time for learning. It's like when townspeople send a child to school. A moran learns much of importance. He learns to defend himself and travel by night. He can bear hunger and he can bear hardship. A man who hasn't served as a moran is not very clever. He is like a child in Europe who has not been sent to school. The men of his age grade do not respect him."

—Maasai

Age Grade

Confused and disrupted is the man who knows not himself. The wisdom of our ancestors in molding and building the soul and spirit of men was great. They developed the age-grade so that men would walk through life in a predictable and meaningful fashion. The warrior must be shown the ways of his creed so that he will not flounder forever in the ways of children. The child is selfish and cares not for the sake of others. His needs must be met and the toiling and suffering of his kindred to meet those needs is of little concern to him. To be uninitiated in the ways of manhood is truly a danger to nation and tribe; for the selfish child will inhabit the body of a man with no purpose in life other than to inflict his childish will upon others. The child, therefore, must be taught to be a man when he is old enough to grasp manhood's significance. Simultaneously, he must be taught the ways of warriorhood; the essence of unselfishness needed to transform the child. After having served, the warrior will retire from the ways of his guild to become an elder and produce children who will carry on the ways and culture of his people.

"Any man can claim to be a hero, but what have you ever done for the kingdom that entitles you to make a claim? Have you ever fought with us against our enemies?...And how have you demonstrated your honor? Have you been kind to helpless people? Do you show respect to old men? Do you give a little food to grandmothers who have no one to care for them? Have you ever carried a bundle of wood for a cripple? Have you ever done anything in your life except abuse the weak?"

—*The hero Bakaridjan Kone in his challenge to a man-beast who sought hero status.*

House of the Warrior

The house of the warrior is a roof resting upon four pillars: Will to Live, Will to Love the Innocent Unconditionally, Will to Protect, and Will to Triumph. If any of these pillars should fail, the roof would be endangered. If only the pillar of Will to Live remained, the warrior would cease to exist and a beast would take his place.

I am the robe which makes the people grand

I am the arrow to their bow

I am the salve which soothes their open wounds

I am the gentle breeze which cools the brow

Or the storm that fiercely rakes the land

For I can be either friend or foe

Attack my flock and you will know

That as warrior I stand

Abyssinian *ras* or noble.

Evil enters like a needle and spreads like an oak tree.

—Abyssinian

By the time the fool learns the game, the players have dispersed.

—Ashanti

A fool and water will go the way they are diverted.

—Abyssinian

Watch the chameleon: it treads ever so carefully, and it can make itself hard to see.

—Zulu

Thinking Through

Know that an attack of an adversary need not always be physical. The greatest conquest is one that gains control of the mind of an adversary thus making it unnecessary to wage war, which is both costly and risky to an aggressor. Once an enemy can twist your perception of reality he need not send troops to seal your fate. The warriors understanding of this will act as an invisible shield against such forces.

"From now on forget the rough ways of moranhood (warriorhood). Don't be rude to junior elders or to any woman. Take with you the good influences of this ceremony. Go home and respect your people. Respect is the most important thing on earth. We are your moral guardians and we take our duties very seriously."

> —*From a Maasai elder's speech at the ceremony of graduation from warriorhood into elderhood.*

"In our traditions we have a code of behavior which emphasizes 'semteende'—reserve and modesty, 'munyal'—patience and fortitude, and 'hakkilo'—care and forethought. This code, along with our many taboos, was given to us by our ancestors."

> —*Wodaabe*

Respect

Be always respectful towards your people. Those who do not nurture the seeds of wrongdoing will always return respect for respect. Respect the cultures and religions of others. All have the right to progress through life as the Creator commands them, unless that culture has proven itself in contention with the laws of righteousness. It is the duty of the custodians of this righteousness to keep such forces in check and, in so doing, protect the balance of earth as it was set from the time of the beginning.

It was dawn when the warriors of my camp came down from the hills
With oxen for the feast.
As we walked along a rise
We looked out over the plain
Where it was said that the earth touched the sky.
We watched as the grass bowed this way, then that way
Unable to resist the gentle voice of the wind
Asking it to dance.
I could barely make out the figure of an elder seemingly in distress
To the west of us.
Atana, our captain bade me go
And look after him.
With a nod, I obeyed and moved swiftly through the plain
My shield knocking rhythmically against my side as I ran.
As I closed the distance between myself and the elder
I could see that he was trying to recapture an ox.
The hills were now painted in gold, amber and shadow
As the solar crown made itself fully known to the landscape.
I drove the haft of my lance into the ground
And leaned my shield against it.
I captured the ox and returned it to the grateful elder
Who spoke of the heroic deeds of his time
As we walked through the grass which bowed this way
Then that way
Heeding the wind as it asked it to dance.

Young Woloff warrior.

"A man may be considered to be a strand of silk within a spider's web. No thread can hang alone; each is linked with its fellows to make a whole. This same thread links a man to his father, to his father's clan and to his ancestors; and others link him to his circumcision brothers. Different ties unite him to the elders who rule the country and administer the law. All these threads come together to form a web, and that web is the society."

—*From Gikuyu mythology.*

The People

The name of the warrior's people is marked in the blood that courses through his veins. Africa is the genesis mother who has extended her reverent mark across the face of the earth. All warriors swear fealty to this mother. Africa is the birthplace of humankind and her children, who still bear the mark of her nurturing sun, possess great power. The warrior seeks this power and uses it for the maintenance of what is just.

"Greetings Mother Earth…
Above you is grain
Beneath you is water
The dead rest on you
The living run on you…
If we plough,
You do not complain of wounds.
Our all-embracing mother…
O *Wondrous Earth!*
Mother full of treasures
We farm and feed from you.
Alive, you carry us.
O *Gratifier of Needs!*
We reproduce on you.
O *Accommodator!*
Be it the perfume-soaked person
With aroma and scent
You extend welcome.
Be it the destitute poor…
You do not reject.
O *Great Leveler!*"

—*From the Oromo Tribute to Mother Earth called the Faarsuu Dache.*

Earth

The warrior to be pure must bond with the Earth. The planet is the Alpha and Omega of life for all things. It is the floor of the House of the Warrior and as such is a gift to all who possess life. Co-existence with all other forms of life is a privilege, which must never be taken for granted or defiled. Remember that the greatest barrier between the servants of right and the servants of disorder is reverence for earth the mother. The warrior must learn to seek the peace and majesty of the fields, mountains and streams by himself and accompanied by his comrades.

"When a male is born, the demon attacks him in the forehead, and as he grows, the demon descends and this man becomes brave, serious and perfect. Then when the demon reaches his feet, he gives him a kick and he is gone. After that he is an honest person who gives beer to the thirsty, food to the hungry, clothes to the naked and haven to the tired."

—*From Abyssinian mythology.*

River

A warrior must be like a river unto his people. He must nourish them when their throats are dry. He must cool them when the heat is too strong. Honor dictates that the warrior must give food to the hungry, heat to the cold, hope to the hopeless, and his shoulder to the fallen. When these things are done well, the people shall flourish.

Do you remember the open plain

Where we saw beyond beyond

Where men were warriors and warriors men

Dignity and honor were precious then

To you do I my hand extend

My brother of the open plain, my friend

Where we saw beyond beyond beyond

Do you my friend remember?

A Hadendoa.

"'My sons, my light is dimming. We will talk further of it, but for now I have something for you to do. Each of you must go out and bring a short stick to me.' The sons went out and returned, each with a short stick. Da Djera said, 'Good. Break your sticks in half.' They did so and Da Djera took the forty-four half sticks and tied them tightly into a bundle. He said, 'Each of you could break a single stick, but can anyone break this bundle?' They tried and no one could break it.

Da Djera said, 'I am going to explain to you the meaning of what we have done. One stick can be broken easily. This is what will happen if you each go your own way alone. Your enemy will break you. But if you stay bound together the enemy can never break you. I want you to pledge now as we sit together, that you will never separate from one another, that you will always be united…'"

—*From an epic of the Kingdom of Segu known as Da Djera and Da Monzon against Samiana Bassi.*

Unity

The warrior is a special breed. Roaming side by side with his warrior brothers through the hills and valleys is the blessed order of his life. The lone warrior can win skirmishes, but the warrior army can win wars. Alone you are strong, united you are a mountain.

"My son I am glad you have come, for very soon now I will go home. The ancestral spirits have given me a clear vision, and I can see you as a mighty tree which, with its branches, will cover the whole country which we know, and many moons journey beyond…But listen carefully to these words, my son. You drink but little of our beer and the hemp-horn of strength (marijuana pipe) you smoke not at all. Why? Because you know that over much beer dulls the mind, and the hemp-horn turns it into a mad bull with much strength but no judgement.

The strongest drink or smoke of all, however, is power. Be careful then to mix it well with mercy, and the reasoning of your councillors and friends, lest it overwhelm you and you become like a mad bull, who, having killed all his opponents, starts goring his defenseless cows and calves and finally charges against the walls of his own kraal (corral) and senselessly breaks his neck instead of walking through the open gate of reason."

—*Zulu King Shaka's stepfather Mbiya addressing him from his deathbed.*

Poisons

Pure is the warrior who neither sells nor uses the mind-altering poisons and blessed is he in the eyes of his forefathers. If you drink that which is fermented, do so only at important celebrations and gatherings. To aid in the distribution of such poison is to surrender to the negative forces around you. To engage in this behavior is to open the floodgates, which would ultimately engulf the innocent.

From the ridge upon which I stood
I could see the cattle of my father's herd
Grazing in the valley below.
I turned and saw the endless sky
Which the elders called the Plains of God
Bathed in red as the sun prepared to set.
I breathed deeply to catch the scent
Of the breeze which now engulfed me
And smelled what I can only call
What is good in life.
I turned once more to descend the hill.
At a stream, I stooped to drink
Extending my hand into the cool waters
Listening to the water's song
As it continued on its ancient path.
When I came nearer the village
I could see young children playing.
They stopped and waved.
One of them, my young cousin ran to me.
She bowed her head in the traditional children's greeting
Then grabbed my hand
And asked countless questions of the warrior's camp
Which had been my home since initiation.
Soon she and the others returned to their play.
I approached my father's herd.
All was well.
My heart soared within my chest
And with each step
I thanked the Creator for this moment
This day
This existence and
This life
As a warrior.

Beja warrior, possibly of Bisharin origin.

"...When the good patriarch become old, his children forgot to follow his pious example, for, from the banana, they had discovered the art of making wine and strong drinks, with which they debauched themselves, and, being daily intoxicated, committed indecencies, became violent in language, reckless and hardened in impiety, and, worse than all, so rebellious as to threaten to depose and kill him. Kintu bore this conduct in his unloving children with meekness and sorrow for a long time, but warned them that their impiety and violence would be punished some day; but they heeded him not, for the wine had maddened them."

—From the Ganda Epic of Kintu, founding hero of Uganda.

Excesses

Engage not in excesses of pleasure whether it be the embrace of women, the drinking of alcohol or eating. The warrior is an example of purity and discipline to the young. As such, the overindulgence in sensual delights is not valid. Such saps the strength and energy necessary for the warrior to succeed.

"Young are the warriors and we feed them the best of our meat. Healthy, they will protect our herds from enemies and famine. And they will stop all the foes of our people from encroaching upon us."

—Sung by senior Maasai warriors to junior ones.

Righteousness

Order and structure are an art and the righteous armed with the chisel of wisdom are the sculptors for human society. The ascendancy of terror, destruction and chaos represent the destruction of balance and justice. Force for the sake of greed or sport flies in the face of righteousness. Warriors serve to sustain or restore balance to their environment and in so doing, become like rain unto the desert.

Without children, the world would come to an end. Without children, the house is sad and silent.

—Swahili

Children speak only words they have heard.

—Yaounde

As you bring your child up, so will it grow.

—Ganda

Children are the profit of life.

—Yoruba

If you want your children to follow in your footsteps, watch where you put them.

—Yoruba

Children

Children are the hope of all nations. By securing their future, you secure your own. Be not profane in their presence and protect them from evil influences. What their people are, they shall become. What you allow them to be subjected to, they will in turn subject their people to. Be as shields unto them and remember that all children of your people belong to you.

My horse was the fastest one of all

Atop my mare I rode—no flew

To each corner of the empire

And charged

Battle after battle

In defense of our lands

On the plains I'd swear she became the wind

And if I lie forgive the sin

Those were great times

Together we saw hill and mountain

Lake, river and thundering fall

We warriors of the saddle rode straight and tall

Bringing honor to our great king's Hall

And my horse was the fastest one of all

Ghogoli of Abyssinia. One of the commanders in a battle with Mussolini's forces on the plains of Welwel in 1934.

"Isaza came to the throne as a young man. He was disrespectful toward the elders whom his father had left to advise him and he drove them away from the palace. He replaced them with lively young men with whom he used to go hunting, his favorite pastime.

One day he killed a zebra and was so pleased with the beauty of the striped skin that he decided to wear it. His companions assisted by sewing the skin and dressing him in it. But as the day wore on, the hot sun dried the skin and it quickly shrank and began to squeeze until Isaza was near death.

He begged his friends for help but they just laughed hard at him and didn't do anything. Of the elders he had driven away, two stayed nearby and Isaza sent to them for help. At first they refused, but then they relented and told Isaza's companions to throw him into a shallow pond.

They did so and the moisture loosened the hide so that it could be removed. In gratitude, Isaza called them back to the palace and gave them a feast reinstating them. At the same time he reprimanded his associates telling them that they should always respect the elders."

—*From the histories of the Nyoro kings.*

Learning

Listen to and learn well from those who are wiser than yourself for they will give you the tools to shape your destiny. They will show you what you need to know to be successful in life. When you become an elder you will be happy to repeat the wisdom of their teachings for you will see how they have served you.

A kind person is the one who is king to a stranger.

—Kongo

A gentleman is recognized even in ragged clothes.

—Swahili

Everyone is polite to a chief, but the man of manners is polite to everyone.

—Kongo

If you offend, ask for pardon, if offended, forgive.

—Abyssinian

Gentleness

Be not harsh of tongue for it is unbecoming of a warrior—a lord among men. It does not hurt to be gentle of speech and slow of anger. The hateful brute is in turn hated but the gentle warrior is much loved.

What makes you run?

Do you run from me?

Is it not the reflection of your soul

You see?

What lies at the end

Of the road you take?

More despair, dishonor, misery, heartache?

Be still and turn

Understand what is true

That you must now transform

To become truly you

Danakil warrior.

If you educate a man, you educate an individual, but if you educate a woman, you educate a family.

—Swahili

The ruin of a nation begins in the homes of its people.

—Ashanti

When a woman is hungry she says, 'Cook something for the children to eat.'

—Swahili

Mother's love is so sweet that you never have enough of it.

—Swahili

Young Women

Recognize the beauty of all women of African blood for they are the mothers of all nations. Respect them at all times for they deserve nothing less. To deceive a woman for the sake of personal pleasure is unacceptable. When you are ready to join the ranks of the elders and create a family, provide for all of the physical and emotional needs of your wife and the children she bears you.

Have your war shield ready while you sit.

—Zigula

If there are enemies about, never go without your club.

—Dama

Watch people's actions. Do not listen to their words.

—Swahili

Snake at your feet, a stick in your hand.

—Abyssinian

Vigilance

The sharp eye of the falcon is the symbol of warrior watchfulness. It is his ever-vigilant presence, seeking signs of internal or external threat, that distinguishes the pure warrior. The natural right of the people to have liberty and peace must not be challenged or threatened.

"An initiated man is adheng (a gentlemen)…his virtue is dheeng (dignity)…elegance, charm, grace, gentleness, hospitality, generosity, good manners, discretion and kindness."

—Dinka

Dignity

When dignity is present in a warrior, he needn't trumpet the fact to others for his very soul will thunder the truth of it for all to bear witness. He who is without it cannot fake it with all of the most skillful boasting in the world. They who are dignified are reserved yet courteous, strong yet gentle, bold yet compassionate. The true warrior walks the land with this manifestation of his inner most strength intact and values it among the highest of all his sacred virtues.

There were warriors once

Men who rode to far flung regions

Through rain and storm

And thoughts of loved ones left behind

There were warriors once

Who braved illness, hunger and death

At the hands of an enemy

All for nothing more

Than the security of their realm

Hard…tough…yet nurturing men

Nurturing enough

To give their lives for the good of the whole

Ah,

Such were the warriors of old!

Cavalryman of the Fulani Sokoto empire.

"Bassadjalan the warrior went to the blacksmith who had forged his magical silver battle staff and said 'You, my blacksmith, I promised you a cow in payment. I have conquered Zanke and taken his cattle. Come and choose the cow you want for yourself.' The blacksmith went with Bassadjalan and chose a cow from the herd. Bassadjalan said 'Take more', but the blacksmith refused saying, 'We spoke of a cow, no more, these were our words and the words of men are the men themselves.'"

—*From the Bambara epic Bassadjalan Zambele and the Heroes of Kala.*

Truth

As the flowers depend upon the sun to rise and nourish them each day, so too will many rely on the warriors. Great is the responsibility that rests with the warrior and he must honor that trust at all times. The word of a warrior must be his bond for lies have no place in a servant of the people. He need not speak on something, which does not have serious implications for the security of others, but he must not lie. This is necessary to enable the people to place trust in their protectors. Therefore, a warrior shall not in any way abridge that trust by engaging in actions, which deceive his people.

"Young men are encouraged to engage in activities which require courage, adventure and endurance without causing distraction or unreasonable risks. They travel far to fell trees for drums; they herd in far off camps for better grass; they hunt wild animals dangerous to livestock and men; they compete in gymnastics and sports; they punish age-mates who disgrace them with moral wrongs; and of course, they defend the land and the herds from aggressors or otherwise substitute their aggressiveness with war songs and dances."

—Dinka

Endurance

The salmon swims upstream, against the current so that it might be able to spawn and ensure the survival of its species. Hardship is an ever-present reality of life as it was established by the Creator longer ago than man can know. Let it not be said that a warrior cannot endure hardship. He must be able to face the obstacles strewn about in this unbalanced state of life. To fail to withstand the rigors of existence is to endanger oneself and the people he serves. The warrior must be prepared to pass these greatest tests of the soul of man. The ability to endure exists in all life although not all are successful in tapping the spring from which it flows. Great is the spirit of the warrior who endures without complaint.

Come dance with me

Come dance the dance of the bold

The dance of honor

The dance of duty

The dance of righteousness

The dance of self control

The dance of truth

I will show you how

For my moves are most skillful

As you see, I dance many dances

And yet my many dances are but one

The dance of the true warrior

An Ashanti warrior demonstrating a hand signal.

Note: *Hand signals used by Ashanti military patrols were adopted by the Boy Scouts by virtue of Boy Scouts founder Baden-Powell having fought against the Ashanti army at the turn of the century.*

"'My son, I do not understand why you have been sitting here all day. What is it you want from me?', asked the blacksmith. Bakaridjan answered, 'My father, I want you to make a knife for me the length of my arm.' The blacksmith said, 'Why were you silent all day? I could have made the knife by now.' Bakaridjan answered, 'My father, when I came I found you busy with your work. I did not want to be disrespectful by interrupting you. So I had patience. I thought a time will come when he will ask me and then I will tell him.' The blacksmith exclaimed, 'Aah, you are an exceptional young man. I will make the knife for you now.'"

—*From the epic of Bakaridjan Kone; a hero of the Bambara kingdom of Segu.*

That Which is Fitting and Seemly

To offend others for no reason is the way of the fool. One should bend over backwards to be polite towards people who have done him no harm. The warrior is civilized, having come from a global tribe with thousands of years of civilization to its credit. When engaged in discussion, wait until the other person has completed their point before interjecting your own. If you know that a person has greater knowledge than you in something, listen and learn. Do not shame yourself by trying to compete with those who hold superior knowledge. Refer to women as "Sister" and to men as "Brother". When stability has been established, elder men should be called "Father" and female elders, "Mother" in order for the circuit of Shaasha to be complete. Do these things and civilized culture shall take root and flourish.

"…certain warriors called the embikas are selected by the warriors for their bravery or maturity…[I]f the cattle needed for milk in the manyattas (war camps) are not donated by the warriors' families, the embikas will take them by force. In general, their duty is to ensure, by any means necessary, that the generation of warriors remains unblemished and of good repute."

—*Maasai*

Integrity

Warriors are servants of uprightness. In order to uphold these principles for the people you serve, you must first uphold them within yourself. Your integrity shall serve as a beacon through the tunnel of corruption and evil. Always maintain this inner sense of that which is good and it will serve you well. To serve evil is to enslave your soul and peace shall never be within your grasp. Expel wrong from your self and do not tolerate it in others.

Questioner:	"'Must then all these beautiful maidens languish and be wasted as potential mothers?'
Shaka:	'A mature woman produces better children than an immature one. Fewer, well-spaced children are better than too many…I tell you all, in future a man will have to prove his worth to be a father, before he receives permission to marry. I will not tolerate the propagation of our race by untried men, who may be undesirable fathers.'"

—From a Zulu "free speech" ceremony where the people were permitted to ask any question of King Shaka Zulu.

Responsibility

Only a child has the right to be irresponsible. He who would make love to a woman and produce a child outside of marriage is no man. The love between man and woman is not sinful, yet to encourage a woman to have your child when you do not have the means or intention of commitment to a family is immoral. With manhood comes responsibility, which cannot be taken lightly lest the people perish under the weight of such offenses. A man should not marry until he is ready. However, if one would foolishly create such a family, he must then provide for it to the ultimate best of his ability.

A thousand torches light the night
And reveal
Regimental banners surfing the night air
And many thousand warriors
Laughing and sharing food and tales
Of deeds past and those to come
All of them united as one
A hush befalls the encampment
And all eyes turn upward
As fire streaks the sky
A sign that victory is at hand
A source of strength to every man
Who will at dawn do his share
Not for glory
Or pay
But for thoughts turned toward children
And families
In the familiar fields of home
And a way of life worth returning to

Zulu warrior holding regimental shield.

Words are like eggs. Once they drop, it's too late.

—Yoruba

Provocation is not good. You should choose what you say.

—Swahili

The word that leaves your mouth leaves your control.

—Somali

Utterances

Let your utterances always show intelligence, eloquence and wisdom. The words of the warrior must be held to a higher standard than those of a child. To speak ill of others of your kind, particularly those who have done you no harm, is a blaspheme against not only your victim but against your bloodline. The warrior must never tolerate the utterance of negative members of his people for words can injure with as much impact as a club. Remember also that such words were probably born from without to impugn the physical beauty, intelligence and strength of your people.

"We brandish spears which are the symbol of our courageous and fighting spirit, never to retreat or abandon hope, or run away from our comrades. If ever we shall make a decision, nothing will change us; and even if the heavens should hold over us a threat to fall and crush us, we shall take our spears and prop it up. And if there seems to be a unity between the heavens and the earth to destroy us, we shall sink the bottom of our spears into the earth, preventing them from uniting; thus keeping the two entities, the earth and the sky, though together, apart. Our faith and our decision never changing shall act as balance."

—From a Gikuyu war song.

Standing Firm

The warrior must stand firm always in the face of adversity. Others may bend but the warrior must plant his feet into the earth and be as the dam that prevents the water from flooding the land. A warrior is a tree among men and as such will be the first target of the ax, which will ultimately dull and break against the bark of his superior soul.

How did they come to us?

Robed in thunder

Shaking the earth with the essence of them.

How did they speak?

In sheets of rain

Bringing nourishment to the life within.

How did they teach?

With billowing flame

Burning the truth

Into the core of our souls.

How went we forward?

In the folds of the wind

Charged with becoming our noblest selves.

How did they leave us?

As burning embers

Awaiting their breath to cause us to blaze.

Barabaig warrior.

"...[O]ur youth is prepared for the manly tasks of the warrior, to venerate our customs, to steel the body, not to allow hand and eye to grow rusty...It is our task, the task of the Loibon [sic] and the elders, to keep the past alive, and bring it into line with our education. Young people are apt to forget easily...The young think that life is nothing but an unbroken chain of pleasure, a calabash of delight which never runs dry...[W]e must tell them, these young men, who they are and where they come from and where their duties lie...[O]ur discipline knew when the time came to stop playing, when limbs and muscles had to perform other tasks than taking girls in a wild embrace."

—*From an interview with a Maasai Laibon (spiritual leader).*

Clearing the Way

The warriors are the advance guard of the people. It is they who must go ahead of the rest and see to it that the proper conditions are present for the establishment of cooperative unity. Once this has been created, stability can begin to take root. Warriors are entrusted with maintaining stability so that the children can grow and thrive as they were meant to.

"Oranyan was a great warrior. In old age, he retired to a beautiful grove and came out only when his people were being attacked, at which time he would defeat the attackers single-handed. One day, however, during a festival, a drunken man called to Oranyan that the people were under attack. Oranyan charged to the scene on a mighty horse, unknowingly killing his own people. The people shouted to him, begging him to stop and see what he was doing. The shocked and heartbroken warrior drove his staff into the ground and promised never to fight again. It is said that he and his staff then turned to stone."

—From the tales of Oranyan, founding hero of the Yoruba nation.

Brotherhood

Truly it is wrong for brother to fight brother. To do so is to attack one's own reflection. This reflection is not your enemy. Your duty as a warrior is to uphold the sanctity of life of the innocent, not to destroy it. Correct those who demonstrate disregard for the well-being and social balance of the people. Extend all opportunities for them to remove themselves from this shameful behavior and in so doing go far beyond what you would deem comfortable.

"There was first of all the Creator. Nothing existed except himself. In order to create the material world, people, animals, trees, plants, grass and all that lives, he divided himself into two principles: the male principle; the inseminator, and the female principle, the bearer. From the combination of these male and female principles, which are opposite, yet one, all life is born. And this is our trinity: God the One, God the Father and God the Mother. For the oneness of God there can be no symbol…The whole earth and all that it bears is the true symbol of God."

—*The Dogon priest Ogotemelli.*

Life

Sacred is the life that has been granted you by the Creator. Man and beast alike fight to keep its flame lit. As the warrior values his life, so must he value the life of all living things. The warrior takes the life of the beast to feed his people as does the lion to feed his cubs. Obey this rule and your feet will be firmly planted on the path.

I may bend but never yield

What wounds are made in time will heal

My trumpet is the clash of steel

With honor as my strongest shield

And with this goes the truth I wield

Do you not see? I will not yield.

Hadendoa warrior, possibly a member of the force that expelled the British from the Sudan in the late 19th century.

"I am ready to die for my country; you know it is better to fight at the frontiers, kill your enemies or die rather than expose your children, your wife and your property to death and ruin."

—Emperor Menelik of Abyssinia

Aggressiveness

Though faced with great challenges, the aggressive warrior will dare the field. Great is the size and power of the wolf, yet the porcupine will triumph over him and cause such pain as to prevent him from returning. Thus, as the wolf avoids the porcupine and the lion avoids the cobra, the intelligent warrior will ultimately achieve success.

"I do not await a second call to leave for the battle front. I hear the news and move out early in the morning."

—From a Dinka war song.

Being Ready

When danger arises, there is no time for sluggishness of feet. Victory belongs to the swift. Mobility is the friend of a warrior. He must never shrink from action. Because there may be much to lose, the warrior must always be on the ready.

Have you not heard the war horns blare

The sound that renders men's souls bare?

Have you not stood upon the hill

With breath so deep and voice so still?

Have you not gazed upon the plain

And viewed the roughly won domain

With memories of battles fought

And too, the freedom that they bought?

Where do you come from? Tell me, where?

Have you not heard the war horns blare?

Nandi warrior.

"Warriors are needed for both simple tasks like capturing a bull, wrestling with one to be branded, and for dangerous ones; protecting the herd from lions or subduing a crazy rhino charging through a kraal. Maasai warriors in their prime seldom fall short in the performance of their duties. When praised, they will answer, 'All we did is what Maasai warriors are to supposed to do.'"

—Maasai

Helping

Beloved is the warrior who acts without question or show of displeasure to the needs of his people, whether to carry the burdensome package of an elder, or to help mend a neighbor's fence, or to retrieve a lost pet. The warrior should delight in the privilege of service to his people. Selfishness is unworthy of the warrior. One who is so inclined imitates the worm that slithers alone through the mud without need of nation or tribe.

A fool and water will go the way they are diverted.

—Abyssinian

Where there is no shame there is no honor.

—Abyssinian

The sun will shine on those who stand before it shines on those who kneel.

—Ibo

Honor

The weak of mind and heart may use drugs to prop them up in their journey through life, but the crutch of the warrior is honor. No job, high office or lucrative post will steer the man without morals from committing wrong. Thieves and dealers of drugs are found from the poorest to the wealthiest of homes. It is honor that transforms beast into man. The warriors' covenant must be in the heart of every warrior. The covenant is between one and one's people but more importantly, between him and his higher self. One's honor must serve as his guide through the sometimes perilous junctures of the river of life. Let no one cause you to break this covenant for it is the truest of all tests of your mettle as a man.

One cut does not bring down a tree.

—Hausa

Do not try your luck once. Try it again and again.

—Zande

Today I do not have it, tomorrow I may get it.

—Dama

The more attempts, the more successes.

—Gikuyu

Persistence

While one blow of the hammer may not break the rock, repeated blows will. A warrior must be persistent in the attempt to achieve his goals. If the first attempt does not accomplish the task, he must try again or change the strategy to gain success.

I am here though you do not see me

You sense my presence when you choose right over wrong

And I am there when you give your hand to one who needs it

I am with you when you honor your word

Yes, I am there when you protect the innocent

And when you try to lift the spirits

Of those who are downtrodden

Even if you do not know them

I leave you when you laugh at the misfortunes of others

And when you hurt those who have not wronged you

But, I return when you show respect to elders

Replace insults with compliments

And think of others before yourself

For I am the ancient warrior who dwells within you

Your twin soul, hoping that one day

You will let me stay

For, think of the new worlds we will explore

When we are joined together as one

A Shilluk of the Sudan.

Maasai Warrior:	"The end of moranhood (warriorhood) is good because you become an elder. People will depend on you. You'll look after their herds and try to find a wife. People rely on elders when they're hungry."
Maasai Elder:	"My children...Disperse to your homes...because we've done our best to organize this ceremony for you. Go now and found villages as we did in our time. Just remember to respect the men who may become your fathers-in-law. You have now entered elderhood."

—A Maasai elder at the Eunoto graduation ceremony.

Elders

A warrior must always respect the elders of his people. The elderly woman or man has earned the right to speak without fear of harsh challenge by the young. If you disagree, do so gently for your ego is not at stake. Do not use elders to prove your skill or knowledge. Elders are the keepers of the great wisdom and as such must always be treated with deference.

"Deed upon deed, honor upon honor, generosity upon generosity, Bakaridjan Kone lived on. His name was known beyond the furthest reaches of the kingdom of Segu. When there were no longer any cities to conquer, no enemies of the king Da Monzon to chastise, no expeditions to lead, still Bakaridjan rode out to demonstrate his valor. Sometimes he was seen in Sahel, sometimes in Sansibara, sometimes in Woroguda, sometimes in Kurusabana, riding a white horse covered with silver trappings, alone except for his faithful servant who rode behind him. Though he had become wealthy from the spoils of wars and gifts of kings, Bakaridjan valued honor and achievement above all wealth. He gave gold to his friends, cowries to the poor and land and cattle to servants…He did not aspire to anything but valor and honor."

—*From the Bambara epic of Bakaridjan Kone, a hero of the ancient kingdom of Segu.*

Fearlessness

Love life but fear not. To serve righteousness is an honor beyond the realm of ordinary life. The warrior true of heart and intention does not perish but lives in the hearts of those for whom he fought. His legacy will dwell in the peace of those whom he saved.

Behold I have come.
Through the mists of the eternal
I have come.
From the inner reaches of radiant expanse
Where shadow is pierced by solar lance
I have come.
For your pain is felt beyond the corridor
And I have come to speak
In the quiet of your mind
So that if you choose
I can help you find
What was lost.
Open your eyes
For a path is laid out before you.
A path of redemption
A path of honor.
Arise
And walk with me
For the ancient ones await your return and…
I
Have
Come
To help you learn
The way.

Hadendoa warrior.

"I remember from my own experience as a warrior how self confidence takes over the whole being, along with pride and a feeling of ease, as if you, yourself and all those around you were thinking 'everything will be all right as long as the warriors are here.' We were supposed to be brave, brilliant, great lovers, fearless athletes, arrogant, wise and above all concerned with the well-being of our comrades and of the Maasai community as a whole. We realized that we were totally trusted by our community for protection, and we tried our best to live up to their expectations."

—Maasai

Confidence

When others doubt, the warrior knows by the truth of his being that victory shall be his. The warrior's resolve must be as sharp and tough as a sword of the finest steel. The guild of the warrior is a spear hurled by the forces of good against the foes of righteousness. It is the mandate of the warrior to overwhelm his adversaries by the strength of his spirit.

"While heir to the throne, Shamba informed his mother that he wanted to travel throughout the land, to see other cultures and learn from them and in the process become wiser. When he returned, he abolished the use of bows and arrows and the shongo, which made horrible wounds. His wisdom and love of peace gained his people respect. If any of his people traveled and were attacked, they need only say that they were Bushongo and the thieves would kneel to them as Shamba's subjects. But if someone was killed by a criminal, the warriors would swarm like locusts to find them. Even then, they were not killed unless they resisted and women and children were always spared."

—Bushongo

Doing Right

The righteous must serve truth even before the people are served. In serving his people the warrior must be sure that their desires are in accord with righteousness. A warrior is a leader and as such, he must hold himself to a high standard. He must not allow the passions of his people to lead him away from what is good. He must hold true to righteous principles for they are a gift from the Creator and are not to be sacrificed even if they put him in violation of earthly commands.

We were roasting beef by the river. Koya, Soran and myself.

The other warriors had gone off on a journey but we remained behind.

We heard the sound of feet running along the trail.

We grabbed our weapons and took positions.

As they came nearer we saw that they were two young boys from a nearby village. When we stopped them, they started speaking excitedly, talking at the same time.

They said that a lion had entered the village during the night and carried off a young calf.

In the process, it had mauled an elder who tried to stop it.

We told them to go back to the village and then headed off.

A lion bold enough to enter a village was a grave threat.

It would wreak havoc in the territory and possibly take many lives if not stopped. We picked up its tracks several miles from the village.

In the distance we saw buzzards circling. We increased our pace and were now running in the direction of the hungry birds.

As we closed the gap we could make out the figure of a black maned male who was not yet aware of us and we could also see the remains of calf's carcass nearby. We slowed to a walk now and balanced our spears. We held our shields in front of us, readying ourselves for a charge. Koya shouted at it. The lion turned and we stood perfectly still. It sniffed the air then looked straight at us. Koya put down his shield and waved his arms over his head. The proud beast had to attack—we understood. Koya quickly picked up his shield and prepared. As the lion got half way to where Koya was waiting, Soran and I let loose our spears—and missed.

The force of the attack knocked Koya off his feet as though he were but a leaf. Before the lion could get around Koya's shield, we had unsheathed our swords

And were on it, slashing like whirlwinds with all the energy we could muster.

After what seemed like an eternity, the lion lay dead and Koya was alive, though bloody

And for all of us, time seemed to have stopped.

With no help, we three had stared death in the face and emerged triumphant.

And we did so not for ourselves but for the safety of the people of our territory.

Thus, we had lived the way we were honored to live.

The warrior's way.

A Lumbwa warrior shown with a slain lion.

"A young warrior happened to be exploring his surroundings while away from his slaughtering camp. He spotted two scouts that had been sent out from his camps to locate any enemy herds of cattle…On the third day, the scouts saw smoke and dust and did not bother to go close enough to see what was causing them…The scouts were sure that the dust was stirred up by cattle and that the smoke was a sign of people present…They returned to the feasting camp and told their comrades how successful they had been…

The young warrior however, was dissatisfied and did not return. He went closer to the smoke and dust only to discover that the dust was caused by stampeding wildebeests coming to a river for water, and the smoke by Ndorobo honey collectors smoking out bees and cooking food.

He walked steadily for one and a half days before he found a suitable source of cattle. The two warriors who had been the official scouts were flabbergasted and refused to accept the young warrior's words. The young warrior's vigilance and honesty, however, were rewarded in the end. Those who followed him were most successful in gaining cattle, while the others failed."

—*Maasai*

Leadership

It is important that a warrior be able to lead as well as follow. A warrior must be able to take initiative if he is reasonably certain that the results of his actions will gain some great benefit. He must be able to assess a situation properly, weigh the consequences, plan the action and then act with decision. All warriors may be tested with leadership from time to time and must be capable of handling such responsibility.

When spider webs unite, they can tie up a lion.

—Abyssinian

A single stick will smoke but it will not burn.

—Galla

A bird may fly in the air but it remembers the ground.

—Mandinka

A family is like a forest, when you are outside it is dense, when you are inside you see that each tree has its place.

—Akan

It takes many trees to make a forest but only one to burn it down.

—Swahili

Loyalty

It is expected that the people be loyal to the common good of the group. To disrespect the sanctity of culture and history is an affront to the responsibilities created in the ancestral forges of time. Walls must be maintained against the corruption of truth or confusion of purpose will result.

You were born with the will to hunt

So hunt...for truth

You were born with the power to choose

So choose...to serve

You were born with your soul in motion

So move...from evil

You were born with the will to fight

So fight...for that which is righteous

You were born with the gift of intellect

So use it...to accelerate wisdom

You were born with the power to discern

So use discernment...for it is the shield of the soul

And if you use all these many gifts...

Then in their using may you rejoice

For you have attained power on the path of warriors

An Oromo warrior.

NGUZO SABA

There were those in our history who took it upon themselves to help restore an African sense of community. Among them was the US organization founded by Maulana Karenga. Although most know of one of their gifts, the institution of Kwanzaa, many have not fully studied the organizing principles upon which Kwanzaa was founded. This is the Nguzo Saba. It is a solid foundation for building a functioning community structure. If Shaasha Barta is a guidebook for governing the behavior of Black men, the Nguzo Saba is a blueprint for structuring the society in which those men must live.

I. Umoja (Unity)—The commitment to the principle and practice of togetherness and collective action on crucial levels i.e., building and maintaining unity in the family, community, nation and race. This is the first and foundational principle because without unity our possibilities as a people are few and fragile, if existent at all.

II. Kujichagulia (Self-determination)—A commitment to the principle and practice of defining, defending and developing ourselves instead of being defined, defended and developed by others. It demands that we build our own image and interests and construct, through our own efforts, institutions that house our aspirations.

III. Ujima (Collective Work and Responsibility)—A commitment to active, informed togetherness on matters of common interest. It is also recognition and respect of the fact that without collective work and struggle, progress is impossible and liberation unthinkable.

IV. Ujamaa (Cooperative Economics)—A commitment to the principle and practice of shared wealth and resources. It grows out of the fundamental African communal concept that the social wealth belongs to the masses of people who created it and that if one should have such an unequal amount of wealth, that it gives him/her the capacity to impose unequal, exploitative and oppressive relations of others.

V. Nia (Purpose)—A commitment to the collective vocation of building, defending and developing our national community in order to regain our historical initiative and greatness as a people. At the core of this principle is, in the final analysis, social purpose, i.e., personal purpose that translates itself into a vocation and commitment which involves and benefits the masses of Black people.

VI. Kuumba (Creative)—A commitment to the principle and practice of building rather than destroying, of positive proactive construction rather than reactive destruction. Inherent in this principle is the commitment to leave our national community stronger, more beautiful and more effective in its capacity to define, defend and develop its interests than when we inherited it.

VII. Imani (Faith)—A commitment to ourselves as persons and a people and the righteousness and victory of our struggle. Moreover, it is belief in and commitment to our brothers and sisters, to their defense and development, and to the fullness of our collective future. Inherent in the principle of Imani is the call for humanistic faith, and earth-oriented, earth-based, people—centered faith in the tradition of the best of African philosophies and values.

About the Author

A discussion of the creation of Shaasha Barta, the Book of the 41 Virtues is aided by some discussion of the author's journey in writing it. The author was born into a household with a fiercely proud Honduran grandfather, descended from Garifuna warriors (also known as the Garinagu), his equally proud and brilliant daughter (the author's mother) and a strong African American father from Maine, himself descended from runaway slaves. Given this mix, a strong sense of self was almost unavoidable. The author's grandfather Tiburcio, a man of regal countenance and powerful intellect, was a pivotal figure in his upbringing and a note about his background would be helpful.

He stressed values above all other things—dignity, honor, respect and fearlessness. This outlook often got him in trouble as a merchant seaman traveling through the Jim Crow south at the turn of the century and landed him in jail after swinging on people who dared to suggest that he move to the back of the bus. In New Orleans after a similar confrontation with a white man, he was persuaded to leave town by local Blacks who assured him that a lynch party would soon arrive.

The history of Tiburcio's people, the Garifuna, is among the most fascinating stories of Blacks in the New World. Historians such as Dr. Ivan van Sertima have identified them as descendants of seafaring Africans, possibly from the Songhay Empire, who arrived prior to Columbus. Some of them established their own society on the island of St. Vincent and became a dominant force there. They formed an alliance with the French against the British for complete control of the island. After a bitter war, the alliance was defeated. Fearful of having the continuing presence of a free Black warrior society in close proximity to their slave plantations, the British exiled the remaining Garifuna to an island called Roatan off the coast of Honduras. The Spanish, having heard of their military prowess, rescued them from exile and resettled them in choice coastal areas in exchange for military service—a service in which they excelled.

Growing up in a predominantly white school within the New York City public school system, the author was stamped intellectually gifted. From there he was targeted by certain teachers for harassment and ultimately became disaffected. At the age of 14, as a high school freshman he took a social studies course, which sent him in an entirely new direction. The course was taught by a white world traveler who, incredibly, taught the truth in a mostly white setting. He stressed that civilization was a gift from Black Africans and he challenged anyone to prove him wrong. Among the pearls he offered was that everything we use, from sidewalks to soap to underwear were innovations of Africans, including the Moors who dominated Spain for over 700 years.

This propelled the author into subsequent research where he discovered the works of W.E.B. DuBois, J.A. Rogers, John G. Jackson and others. Ironically, this ruined his high school career as a result of his spending more time at the Schomburg Library in Harlem than in school. This new track also led him to Alkebu-Lan Books, the publishing home of Dr. Yosef ben Yochannan, where he quietly volunteered in his spare time and was helped in his studies by a man named Greg Hardy who would give him books by "Dr. Ben" to take home and read.

Many years later, while working as a counselor with incarcerated juvenile felons, the author became acutely aware of the need for guidance on the part of these young men. The vast majority were raised without fathers and those who did have fathers had received no guidance of any value from them. It was also clear that their dilemma was simply a microcosm of the dilemma of Black males in America—no functional values and no repositories of wisdom. Equally important, there were no conduits for life affirming and enhancing culture tailored to their developmental needs.

Several of the author's co-workers at the detention facility were continental Africans. It was quite interesting to observe the relative wholeness of the Africans, which was evident in the intensity of their intellect, their humanity, courtesy, kindness and wisdom. In fact, the author noticed early on that these character traits reminded him very strongly of his grandfather.

During his organizing activities, the author often spoke to young Black males on street corners, many of them drug dealers who, far from being hostile as is the common perception, were hungry for some kind of interaction with people interested in their welfare. This book is for them and all Black males everywhere who struggle to regain their balance.

Notes

1. F. Deng, <u>The Dinka of the Sudan</u>. New York. Holt, Rhinehart and Winston. 1972, p.21.

2. T. Saitoti, <u>Maasai</u>. New York. Harry N. Abrams, Inc. 1981, p.111.

3. H. Courlander and O. Sako, <u>The Heart of the Ngoni: Heroes of the African Kingdom of Segu</u>. New York. Crown. 1982, p.6.

4. J. Maquet, <u>Civilizations of Black Africa</u>. New York. Holt, Rhinehart and Winston. 1972, p.117.

5. <u>Maasai Manhood</u>. Produced by Granada Television for Public Broadcasting. 1980.

6. F. Deng op. cit., p.13.

7. Courlander and O. Sako op. cit. p.5.

8. J.A. Hunter, <u>Hunter</u>. New York. Harper and Brothers. 1952, p.103.

9. Ibid. p.104.

10. J. Jordon, <u>Elephants and Ivory</u>. New York. Rhinehart and Company. 1956, p.64.

11. E.A. Ritter, <u>Shaka Zulu</u>. New York. Penguin Books. 1978, p.23.

Bibliography

Abraham, W.E., The Mind of Africa. Chicago. Chicago University Press, 1962.

Black Man's Land. Produced by Anthony David Productions for PBS, 1972.

Brown, J.M., Kenyatta. New York. E.P. Dutton and Co. 1973.

Courlander, H. and Sako, O., The Heart of the Ngoni: Heroes of the African Kingdom of Segu. New York. Crown 1982.

Davidson, B., The African Genius. Boston. Atlantic-Little, Brown 1969.
A History of East and Central Africa. Garden City, New York. Anchor. 1969.
A History of West Africa. Garden City. Anchor 1966.

Deng, F., The Dinka of the Sudan. New York. Holt Rhinehart and Winston 1972.

Erlich, H., Ras Alula and the Scramble for Africa. Lawrenceville, N.J. Red Sea Press 1996.

Hunter, J.A., Hunter. New York. Harper and Brothers 1952.

Jordon, J., Elephants and Ivory. New York. Rhinehart and Company 1956.

Knappert, J. The A-Z of African Proverbs. London. Karnak House 1989.

Koenig, O., The Masai Story. London. Michael Joseph LTD 1956.

Maquet, J., Civilizations of Black Africa. New York. Holt Rhinehart and Winston 1972.

Omoyela, O. and Lindfors, B., Yoruba Proverbs. Ohio. Center for International Studies—Ohio University 1973.

Osoba. F., Benin Folklore. London. Hadada Ltd. 1993.

Parrinder, G., <u>African Mythology</u>. London. Hamlyn Publishing Group 1967.

Ritter, E.A., <u>Shaka Zulu</u>. New York. Penguin Books 1978.

Saitoti, T., <u>Maasai</u>. New York. Harry N. Abrams, Inc. 1981.

Seabrook, W., <u>Jungle Ways</u>. New York. Harcourt Brace and Co. 1931.

Stanley, H.M. <u>Through the Dark Continent</u>. Vol. I. New York. Dover 1988.

Zelalem Aberra, <u>Sagalee Haraa</u>. Vol. 14. United Kingdom. 1996.

0-595-28975-4

Printed in the United States
29787LVS00003B/303

9 780595 289752